*Wishing learning joy to every student
and teacher, especially my grandchildren,
Ben, West, Monae, and East*
—JH

For Thomas and William
—KH

Text copyright © 2014 by Janet Halfmann
Illustrations copyright © 2014 by Katy Hudson
All rights reserved/CIP data is available.
Published in the United States 2014 by
🍎 Blue Apple Books, 515 Valley Street,
Maplewood, NJ 07040
www.blueapplebooks.com
First Edition
Printed in China 08/14
ISBN: 978-1-60905-391-8
1 3 5 7 9 10 8 6 4 2

Janet Halfmann

Animal Teachers

illustrations by
Katy Hudson

BLUE APPLE

Who taught you how to do things?

Your parents and others who care about you were your first teachers.

Who teaches animals?

Let's peek into some animal lessons and find out!

Food Lessons

Baby chicks peck at everything, even their toes. So Mama Hen conducts food lessons.

First, the chicks take seeds right from Mama's beak. Then she drops seeds for her little ones to pick up. Soon the baby chicks know seeds from toes and are pecking their way to full stomachs.

Who taught you what's good to eat?
Did you ever try to bite your toes?

Swimming Lessons

Baby Sea Otter will live mostly in the water. So Mama Otter gives him swimming lessons.

Mama Otter plops her pup on his belly, then swims just ahead. Pup paddles wildly to catch up with Mama. When he does, she gives him a kiss. Later, she'll teach him how to dive deep down to the bottom of the sea.

Who gave you your
first swimming lessons?
Can you swim now?

Boxing Lessons

Joey Kangaroo
will live among a
rough-and-tumble troop.
So Mama Kangaroo
conducts boxing lessons.

Pow, pow! Kick, kick! Joey play-boxes with Mom
and other young kangaroos. He pushes with his front paws
and kicks with his big hind feet. By the time he grows up,
he'll be ready to defend himself.

How do you
defend yourself?
Do you use your words—
or your feet?

Building Lessons

Beaver Kits will someday make their own homes. So Mama Beaver conducts building lessons.

Day after day, little beaver kits work side by side with parents and older brothers and sisters. They cut down trees and dig canals. They add to the lodge and fix the dam. By the time beavers are two years old, they are on their own and know how to build their own water world.

Have you ever built something with sticks, or blocks, or mud? Can you make a fort or castle to play in?

Drinking Lessons

Baby Elephant's trunk can do many things. So Mama Elephant gives her drinking lessons.

Baby Elephant watches her mom suck up water with her trunk and squirt it into her mouth.

When Baby tries, she blows bubbles
and splashes water everywhere.
With practice, Baby will get it right.
She will join her herd for a drink
at the elephant watering hole.

Can you drink from a water fountain?
Did you ever splash yourself
or get water up your nose?

Shouting Lessons

Prairie Dog Pups
live in big groups called towns.
They have to know how to be
heard among the crowd.
So prairie dog parents
give them shouting lessons.
Chee-chee! Yip-yip!
Wee-oo! Wee-oo! Wee-oo!

Prairie dog pups copy the adults, jumping up and yipping at the sky—

Wee-oo! Wee-oo! Wee-oo!

Soon they'll learn all the yips and barks that echo through the prairie dog town. Each pup will know how to say, "Watch out!" or "All is clear!"

Do you yip? Can you bark?
Or shout? Or yelp?
How do you make
yourself heard?

Nut-Cracking Lessons

Baby Chimps
need to be able to eat all
the good food in the forest.
So Mama Chimp gives
nut-cracking lessons.

In the rain forest of West Africa,
little chimps watch their mamas
lay hard nuts on one stone and
whack them with another.
One little chimp borrows Mama's "hammer."
She pounds and pounds and pounds.
Crrr-acck!
The nut is open. Yum!

Can you crack open
a walnut or pecan?
What is your
favorite nut?

Singing Lessons

Penguin Chicks stay in a huge penguin nursery while their parents are away. To help parents find their chicks among the crowd, the mother and father give singing lessons.

Emperor Penguin Chick listens closely to learn the song of his parents
before they leave to get fish to eat. When the mamas and daddies return,
they'll sing their songs to the huge huddle of hungry chicks.
It will be up to each penguin chick to pop up from the crowd and say,
"Here I am!"

Are you a good singer?
Who sings to you?

Keeping Dry

Baby Orangutan
lives in a wet, rainy forest.
So Mama Orangutan gives
lessons on how to keep dry.

Splish-splash-splish!
Raindrops fall on Baby Orangutan.
She doesn't like getting wet!
Mama gathers lots of leafy branches.
She places the pile over both their heads
to create a big green umbrella.
Before long, Baby Orangutan knows how to keep
herself dry in the rainy, splishy-splashy rain forest.

Have you ever used your backpack
as a hat when caught in the rain?
Ever shared an umbrella?
What do you wear to keep dry
on rainy days?

Running Lessons

Baby Cheetahs grow up to be the fastest animals on land. So Mama Cheetah gives them running lessons.

Mama brings small animals home for the cheetah cubs to chase.
When they grow older, they follow Mama on the hunt.
They copy her every move, learning to stalk, spring, and sprint.

Are you a fast runner?
Have you ever chased something?
Do your parents ever run after you?

Learning Mama's Name

Bottlenose Dolphin
needs to learn to "talk" like his mother.
So Mama Dolphin gives him whistling lessons.

Right after Baby Bottlenose Dolphin is born,
Mama whistles and whistles. *Eeeeeee! Eeeeeee!*
She is repeating a special whistle all her own.
It says, "This is me!"

Soon, Baby can find Mama by her whistle. Or he can call for her
by using it himself. Mama's whistle-name sounds out through the
water of the sea, helping keep mother and baby close.

How old were you when you said
your first word?
Was it "mama" or "daddy" or "grandma"?
Do you ever whistle
to get someone to notice you?

Fishing Lessons

B aby Bear
needs to eat a lot to grow big and strong.
So mother bear gives him fishing lessons.

A brown bear cub follows his mother into the stream. She stares at the water.
POUNCE! She pins a fish with her paws, then puts it in her mouth.
The cub tries to fish, too. It's hard.
Too slippery! Too fast! Finally, SUCCESS!
Bear Cub grabs his fish and sprints to shore. Now it's dinnertime!

Have you ever
gone fishing?
Did you catch a fish
on the first try?

More Animal Facts

Chickens
- A mother hen turns the eggs that she is sitting on many times a day. This keeps the yolks from sticking to the shells.
- When chicks peep while inside their shells, their mother hen clucks back to them.
- Chicken eggs can be white, brown, blue, green, or even pink.

Sea Otters
- Sea otters sleep on their backs on top of the water.
- To keep from floating away while they sleep, a mother otter often wraps herself and her pup in seaweed for the night.
- An otter lays a flat stone on its stomach to crack open the shells of crabs and clams.

Kangaroos
- Joeys also play-box with bushes.
- Kangaroos are good swimmers.
- Kangaroos use their large, strong tails to balance when they hop.

Beavers
- Baby beavers are born with teeth. Their teeth never stop growing.
- Beavers can stay underwater 15 minutes without coming up for air.
- Beavers have a set of see-through eyelids that work like goggles underwater.

Elephants
- A baby elephant sucks on its trunk like a human infant sucks its thumb.
- An elephant calf is the biggest baby born on land.
- At one day old, an elephant calf can walk almost a mile.

Prairie Dogs
- The prairie dog is a member of the squirrel family. It gets its "dog" name from its "bark."
- Prairie dogs greet one another by touching their front teeth together.
- The high dirt mound around a prairie dog burrow serves as a lookout point and keeps out water.

Chimps

- Baby chimps, like human babies, love to be rocked.
- Chimps walk on the knuckles of their hands and the flat soles of their feet.
- Newborn chimps have pink skin that turns black as they grow up.
- Chimps often laugh when they play and giggle when they're tickled!

Emperor Penguins

- The father emperor penguin balances the egg on his feet.
  His lower belly has a cozy pouch to keep the egg warm.
- While caring for their eggs, emperor penguin fathers huddle together.
  They take turns moving to the warmer center of the huddle.
- Adult emperor penguins can go without eating for more than four months.

Orangutans

- The orangutan builds a new sleeping nest in the trees every night.
- Young orangutans have to learn to find 300 different kinds of fruit!
- Orangutans' arms are longer than their bodies.

Cheetahs

- Cheetahs are the fastest land animals. They can sprint 70 miles per hour—
  that's as fast as a car driving at top speed on a highway!
- Cheetahs can't roar like lions and tigers.

Bottlenose Dolphins

- Dolphins sleep by shutting down half their brain. They often sleep with one eye open.
- Dolphins look like fish, but they are mammals. They breathe air like people do.
- Dolphins like to ride on waves made by boats.

Brown Bears

- Baby bears are born while their mother is asleep in her winter den.
- Newborn cubs are blind, have little hair, and weigh only as much as
  a pound (four sticks) of butter.
- A brown bear's sense of smell is seven times better than that of a bloodhound.